A Note to Parents

DK READERS is a compelling program for beginning readers, designed in conjunction with leading literacy experts, including Dr. Linda Gambrell, Distinguished Professor of Education at Clemson University. Dr. Gambrell has served as President of the National Reading Conference, the College Reading Association, and the International Reading Association.

Beautiful illustrations and superb full-color photographs combine with engaging, easy-to-read stories to offer a fresh approach to each subject in the series. Each DK READER is guaranteed to capture a child's interest while developing his or her reading skills, general knowledge, and love of reading.

The five levels of DK READERS are aimed at different reading abilities, enabling you to choose the books that are exactly right for your child:

Pre-level 1: Learning to read
Level 1: Beginning to read
Level 2: Beginning to read alone
Level 3: Reading alone
Level 4: Proficient readers

The "normal" age at which a child begins to read can be anywhere from three to eight years old. Adult participation through the lower levels is very helpful for providing encouragement, discussing storylines, and sounding out unfamiliar words.

No matter which level you select, you can be sure that you are helping your child learn to read, then read to learn!

DK

LONDON, NEW YORK, MUNICH,
MELBOURNE, and DELHI

Designer Sandra Perry
Jacket Designer Lauren Rosier
Design Manager Ron Stobbart
Publishing Manager Catherine Saunders
Art Director Lisa Lanzarini
Publishing Director Alex Allan
Pre-Production Producer Andy Hilliard
Producer Louise Daly
Reading Consultant Dr. Linda Gambrell

First published in the United States in 2012
by DK Publishing
375 Hudson Street, New York, New York 10014
10 9 8 7 6 5 4 3 2 1

LEGO and the LEGO Logo are trademarks of The LEGO
Group.
Copyright © 2012 The LEGO Group
Produced by Dorling Kindersley
under license from The LEGO Group

Page Design Copyright © 2012 Dorling Kindersley Limited

001—186375—Oct/12

DK books are available at special discounts when purchased
in bulk for sales promotions, premiums, fund-raising,
or educational use.
For details, contact:
DK Publishing Special Markets
375 Hudson Street
New York, New York 10014
SpecialSales@dk.com

A catalog record for this book is available
from the Library of Congress.

ISBN: 978-0-7566-9849-2 (Paperback)
ISBN: 978-0-7566-9850-8 (Hardcover)

Color reproduction by Media Development and Printing, UK
Printed and bound in USA by Lake Book Manufacturing, Inc.

Discover more at
www.dk.com

www.LEGO.com

Contents

DK READERS

READING
3
ALONE

LEGO **MONSTER FIGHTERS**

Watch Out, Monsters About!

Written by Simon Beecroft

Welcome to Monsterland

Welcome, fellow monster hunters. You join us on a perilous quest to a dark and scary land where ghoulish creatures rule, and mortals and minifigures are most unwelcome. You will encounter creatures from your nightmares: Werewolves, ghosts, vampires, and worse! But remember, you are not alone. You are part of a band of hardy explorers. Together we are the Monster Fighters!

Who am I? Dr. Rodney Rathbone, of course. I will be your guide on this journey into fear. Do you have your sword at the ready? Then let's go...

Monsters and Moonstones

Our present mission all began with a curious jewel known as a Moonstone. An evil mastermind, Lord Vampyre, learned of the jewels' powerful magic. If he can gather six Moonstones, he will be able to harness their power.

The Crazy Scientist

The Zombie Groom

The Werewolf

Then darkness will
cover the whole world!
So Lord Vampyre
mounted a search for every
Moonstone in the Monster World.
They are guarded by ghoulish creatures
in places few minifigures dare to go.

Ghost

The Mummy King

Lord Vampyre

The Swamp Creature

The Crazy Scientist's Monster

The Monster Fighters

We must take the Moonstones before Lord Vampyre can get his undead hands on them. Time is short. The monsters are very close to collecting the remaining stones and there is only one hope left. I have assembled a team of heroes who won't let the lights go out without a fight. Major Quinton Steele, Frank Rock, Jack McHammer, and Ann Lee: Together we are the Monster Fighters!

Join us if you dare.

Frank Rock

Ann Lee

Quinton
Steele

Jack McHammer

9

Dr. Rodney Rathbone

As you know, I am the leader of this quest to save the world. But who am I? I am an aristocrat, an adventurer, and the great-great-great-grandson of the first minifigure ever to step foot into the Monster World.

My story began in jolly old London, where I spent my youth fencing and writing journals.

Monster fighting is in my blood. I'll never forget my first scrap with a vampire—I lost my leg (now a mechanical replacement). But nothing will stop me riding my Midnight Bike into the next adventure...

Enter the Vampyre

Do you have an archenemy?
All adventurers should
have one! My archenemy
is none other than Lord
Vampyre. He rarely
leaves his castle, but
when he does, he
travels in his hearse,
driven by Renfield,
his Zombie Driver.

Lord Vampyre's funeral hearse is
powered by the Vampyre Moonstone.
This makes it supernaturally fast!
Many times, I've given chase in my
Midnight Bike. I've even grabbed
that magical jewel. Trouble
is, Lord Vampyre keeps
stealing it back!

Major Quinton Steele

But enough about my exploits. Let me tell you about my fellow Monster Fighters, starting with Major Quinton Steele. He's a big-game hunter with a thirst for exotic prey. The Major was born in South Africa and has traveled to every corner of the world.

He is an expert in every kind of hunting, tracking, and combat skill. His vehicle of choice is a Safari Buggy and he carries a big rifle with telescopic sight. (He also has a telescopic eye!)

Major Steele carries werewolf teeth on his belt as hunting trophies.

The Werewolf

When I first met Major Steele, he was searching for a new hunting challenge in places where few other minifigures would dare to go. He told me, "I'm going to stop that Werewolf's tail from wagging!"

Venturing into the wild wood, he spotted a Werewolf Moonstone. As he approached, the snarling Werewolf leapt out at him. It was an ambush! The Major wanted action—now he had it...

Spiky Beast
The Werewolf haunts the deep, dark forest of the Monster World. His fangs are sharp and he NEVER cuts his claws!

Monsters and Scientists

There are some places that should never be entered alone! The Crazy Scientist's laboratory is one of them. That's why Major Steele and I went together in the Monster Buster.

I had heard rumors of what went on in there: Brewing potions, creating spells, and breeding rats and spiders for ghoulish experiments. But we were unprepared for the true horror of what we saw...

It was a hideous green monster lying on a bench. Massive energy beams were being fired into its head. Suddenly, with a terrifying jolt, it came alive!

Crazy Scientist
No experiment is too dangerous or crazy for this crazy wizard. He even turned his own hair white and made it stand on end!

Escape from the Lab

The Crazy Scientist's Monster came after us with superhuman strength. I did what any expert adventurer would do. I grabbed the Moonstone and dashed out of there.

It was only when I was a mile or two away that I noticed something amiss. Major Steele wasn't with me! I had left him behind!

The Monster is held together with safety pins and tape

Dungeon crawling with creepy bugs

In my excitement, I had not noticed that the Scientist had captured the Major and locked him in his dungeon. So then I had to break him free. No adventure is simple!

Frank Rock

My fellow adventurer, Frank Rock, is a rebel out for revenge. I found him traveling in search of his missing dog, who he believed had been stolen by slimy ghouls. Frank has had a grudge against Swamp Monsters ever since.

Where was Frank born? I've never found out. All Frank says is he lives on the wild side. With his swamp boat, pistols, and dark glasses, the Swamp Creature had better head for dry land—and hide!

Battle in the Swamp

Frank knows just where the Swamp
Creature lives: In the stinkiest part of
the slimiest swamp in the whole of
the Monster World. Frank Rock has
sworn not to shave his stubble or
remove his sunglasses until he has the
Moonstone in his yellow hands.

When Frank goes into battle, he goes in with all his flick-firing missiles blazing. Frank's only rules in combat are: Break all the rules and walk away from explosions without looking back at them!

Frank's not scared of any monsters—only of a bad hair day!

Ann Lee

Ann Lee is a magician and monster-basher who is ready for anything. I discovered her while I was looking for a pilot brave enough to fly an aircraft into the Monster World. She was there in the aircraft hangar, secretly practising her martial arts.

I don't know where Ann is from or where she trained. But she can pilot any flying vehicle and is an expert shot with her crossbow. (She even uses spare ammo as a hair accessory!)

Ann carries garlic cloves and wooden stakes on her belt—Vampires had better go crying back to their coffins!

The Mummy's Curse!

The Mummy King likes to put curses on minifigures, but curses can be slow... Swords are faster!

The Mummy Battle

I discovered that the dreaded Mummy King was planning to deliver his precious Moonstone to Lord Vampyre. So I sent Ann Lee to intercept his ghostly chariot, which I knew was protected by magical curses and pulled by a creepy skeleton horse. Ann swooped down in her steamcopter. She used her magic skills to break the Mummy's protective curses. The Moonstone was hers for the taking... if only she could get past the Mummy King himself!

The Ghost Train

Ann Lee and Frank Rock make a daredevil team. Together they went after a Moonstone guarded by Ghosts on a flying Ghost Train! Frank took the controls of the acrobatic stunt plane, the Monster Fighter Wing, and the fearless Ann swung underneath it on a chain! Steady does it, Anne—avoid the ghosts and the Moonstone will be yours!

The Ghosts

The three ghouls that haunt the Ghost Train glow in the dark. They even carry their own weapons, too!

Captured by Ghosts

When you are a Monster Fighter, things often don't go as planned. Ann Lee had been close to capturing the Ghost Moonstone, when the wailing Ghosts captured her! They locked her in a prison wagon, with bars made of bones! Luckily, Frank Rock came to her rescue. He didn't realize that it was really Anne's magical powers that opened the prison bars!

(Don't tell Frank, will you? He does like to be the hero.)

Jack McHammer

Jack McHammer is a burly lumberjack.
He's built like the trunk of an oak
and was born in the backwoods of
Scotland... or perhaps Canada. Jack
never leaves home without his
hammer—and his manly red beard.

Hammer basher

Jack lost his right arm in a fight with a monster years ago, and he's still angry about it. He drives a Hammer Truck, which has green missiles and giant hammer weapons. When I met Jack, I knew I had just the match for a Zombie Horde...

Powerful engine

Monster catcher

Zombie Graveyard

One of the trickiest Moonstones to capture is located on a spooky tomb in a ghoulish graveyard.

All around is swirling green mist, strange noises, glowing spiders, and bloodsucking bats. But secrets lurk in dusty graves and ancient tombs…

These graves are home to Zombies!
A Zombie Bride sleeps beneath the
Moonstone tomb. A Zombie Groom
and his undead Chauffeur haunt
graves on either side.

This is a misssion that has Frank
McHammer's name on it...

Zombies Attack!

When Jack McHammer goes after a Moonstone, he doesn't waste time planning a clever plan of attack. Jack just walks in and takes it. He may be a plastic hotshot with the might of ten minifigures, but he's not subtle!

Jack gets the Moonstone, but he's woken up the Zombies. Rising from their graves, the Zombie Groom, the Zombie Bride, and the Zombie Driver will do anything to protect their Moonstone. Luckily, Jack is a minifigure who likes a fight...

Moonstone Crisis

Despite our best efforts, that dastardly Lord Vampyre has somehow got hold of all six Moonstones! As the stars align in the night sky, Lord Vampyre and his Vampyre Bride prepare to unite the Moonstones and use their power to eclipse the Sun.

He has built a machine in his Vampyre Castle in which to place the Moonstones. The castle is well protected and full of traps. Lord Vampyre must be stopped!

Moonstone Machine

Deadly Device
Lord Vampyre's Moonstone Machine sends out a powerful energy beam that moves the Moon right in front of the Sun!

Vampyre Castle

I had to confront my archenemy. I went with Frank McHammer, knowing that only his strength and my brains would save the day.

We arrived at the castle in the dead of night. First we had to defeat Lord Vampyre's demonic Manbats. While I distracted them with my sword and pistol, Frank edged closer in the Monster Buster. Then he fired the net... Take that, you flying, fanged beasties!

Inside the Castle

Once inside the castle, Frank and I
had to face new terrors. The Vampyre
Bride welcomed us with cocktails.
But green potions
don't agree
with me.

*Bubbling
green poison*

So we gave the Vampyre Bride the slip. Frank led her on a wild goose chase around a revolving spiral staircase.

Meanwhile, I reached a secret map room at the top of a tall tower. Suddenly, a trap door opened beneath my feet and I fell to the spikes below. As luck would have it, I landed on my metal leg and this saved me from certain death!

The Final Showdown

Finally, Jack and I reached the
Moonstone Machine and removed
the Moonstones. But a Manbat flew
at Jack with its fangs bared. Then a
black shadow swooped down toward
me. It was Lord Vampyre himself,
armed with a fearsome black sword.
I drew my sword and we fought...

Clash, bash! Our swords struck each other. Take that you toothy terror! This time I won. But next time—who knows!

Menacing Phantom
Some monsters never die. Lord Vampyre will return. You can be sure of that!

Glossary

Align
When things move into a special position.

Ammo
Short for ammunition; things you can fire at an enemy, such as arrows and bullets.

Archenemy
A chief enemy.

Aristocrat
A member of the ruling class of people in society.

Big game
Large animals that are hunted or fished for sport.

Bride
A woman who has recently got married.

Chariot
An ancient horse-drawn two-wheeled vehicle.

Chauffeur
Someone who is paid by someone else to drive them around in their car.

Cocktail
A mix of different drinks.

Crossbow
A weapon consisting of a bow fixed crosswise on a wooden handle, with grooves along the handle to direct an arrow.

Curse
A wish that someone else has nothing but bad luck or misfortune.

Dastardly
Mean and cowardly.

Eclipse
When one object in space, such as a sun or moon, moves in front of another, so that to an observer the one in front blocks out the one behind.

Exploit
An act or deed, especially a brilliant or heroic one.

Fencing
The art or sport of using a thin bladed sword in attack and defense.

Ghost
The spirit of a dead person which appears as a floating presence.

Groom
Short for bridegroom; a man who has recently been married.

Hangar
A shelter for housing or repairing aircraft.

Hearse
A vehicle for carrying a coffin to a church or cemetery.

Laboratory
A place where scientific experiments take place.

Martial arts
Any of various arts of self-defence and techniques of single combat, such as judo or karate, originating in Asian countries such as Japan and China.

Mastermind
A person with outstanding intelligence.

Mortal
An ordinary human being with no super powers.

Mummy
In Ancient Egypt, a person or animal wrapped in bandages to preserve their dead body.

Stake
A piece of wood or metal with a point at one end.

Stunt plane
An airplane that does spectacular manoeuvres, such as loops or rolls.

Supernatural
Something that does not normally exist in nature.

Werewolf
A person who becomes a human-sized wolf every full moon.

Vampire
A dead person who comes back to life and bites their victims to drink their blood.

Zombie
A dead person who comes back to life. When they attack others they can turn them into zombies!